Cornish Sayings Superstitions and Remedies

*Cornwall will stand
a shower every day
and two on Sunday*

Originally published March 1973
Reprinted February 1975, July 1981, May 1987

New revised edition 2006

Published by Truran, Croft Prince, Mount Hawke, Truro,
Cornwall TR4 8EE
www.truranbooks.co.uk
Truran is an imprint of Truran Books Ltd

ISBN-10 **1 85022 204 5**
ISBN-13 **978 185022 204 0**

Printed and bound in Cornwall by R Booth Ltd,
Antron Hill, Mabe, Penryn, Cornwall TR10 9HH

Cornish Sayings Superstitions and Remedies

Compiled by
KATHLEEN HAWKE

truran

Cornish Sayings

Going at it like a bull at a gate

'Tez so broad's 'tez long

They wuz having a proper slinging match (dispute)

She'd skin a flea for a farthing

For pity's sake stop gulging, you'll chuck yerself (eating quickly; choke)

She's a proper wild-de-go (rash; reckless)

Dressed up like a lawyer

Bossed about like stinking fish

Looking like a dying duck in a thunderstorm

Like a fly in a jam pot (can't keep still)

Wear pink to make the boys wink

Can't blow nor strike (perplexed)

I forgot myself (went to sleep)

Worse than a flea to catch (never home)

It's a sin to steal a pin, let alone a bigger thing

Healthy as a trout

We don't pull and drag Sundays (shake mats)

Like a toad under a harrow (weighed down)

Straight as a pound of candles (good character)

The old must go, the young may go

Flowers fade on flirts

Gulls crying were said to be the souls of men crying to be saved

Aw gate knaw nothing gwain nowhere (stupid person)

Always ill and sickly, more
likely to live than die quickly

Hung up his hat (said of a
young man invited to supper
by his lady love)

*Deaf on one ear
and can't hear
on the other*

Going like a lamplighter

You'd think money grew upon ferns
(said of a spendthrift)

Take yer hands out yer pockets, they'll look like want
catchers' pockets (want-mole)

Will 'ee have a drop of warm? (tea)

Hitched up (said of children not looked after)

Looking like a winnard (looking cold)

The poor soul was in some taking (upset)

As drunk as a Piraner

Pride is never cold

As good as a Christmas play

Three on one horse like going to Morvah Fair

Don't know and won't be told

Strong in the hand, weak in the head

If there's any difference they're both alike

The Lord will provide, if He doesn't He isn't to His
promises

*Lost your appetite and found
a donkey's
Running round like a
scalded cat*

As bowld as brass
As old as the hills
Oal of a dither
Black as a tinker
Drunk as m'lord
Limp as a dish-rag or dish-clout
Near as the grave
Tough as ole Sir Nick
Dear as saffron
Standing in his awn light like the Mayor of Market Jew
Grizzlin' like a badger gwain to faist
They that caan't schemey must louster
Too slow to carry cold dennar
Like Lady Fan Todd, dressed to death and killed with
    fashion.
Goin' up like 'smawk' (smoke)
Com in' down like rain
He looks as if a good meal's meat would do him good
Thin as a griddle
Back like a barn door

Backwards an' forwards like
    Boscastle Feer (Fair)
Like Lanson gaol, oal upside down
    (Launceston)
Like Tregonetha Fair, nigh by and
    handy
All aboard like Perran singers

Wan of Pharaoh's lean kind

Head like a turmot

Feet like hafe-crown shovels

Behind like a butter-tub

Like two hellens (slates) clapped together

As thin as a rushlight

Like a bundle of straw tied in the middle (fat person)

As thin as a rake

Wha's oal tha pore weth ee? (What's all the hurry?)

Busy as batty, dawn't knaw which way to steer nor turn

Eyes as black as sloanes (sloes)

Fit like a mungern (straw horse collar)

Dry as a boot

Taties and point (point to the meat)

Tough as Hancock's mother

Black as your hat

Ne'er cast a clout till May is out

Shaking like a apsen leaf (aspen)

'Tedn' all the world nor half a parish

Sweating like a poultice

As plain as a pikestaff

Rusty as a anchor

Childrens' tongues will cut your throat with a bar of soap, or hang you with a yard of cotton

Like Tregony band, three scats behind

At Poldice the men are like mice

Like the Mayor of Calenick who rode two miles to walk one

Clear as you go and you'll never be in a fouch (muddle)

Nuffs nuff, too much is a feast

As poor as a coot

As cunning as a fox

As stupid as an owl

You'd think she was brought up in Court, pigs one end and
she t'other, (said of a proud person)

Black as a turf-rick toad

Towsers in one generation, towsers again in the third

Full as a egg

Empty plates, full bellies

Good health is a merry meal

Put the wood in the hole (shut the door)

Always on the ran dan (never home)

Gone into a decline (suffering from tuberculosis)

Sewed on with a red hot needle and burning thread (loose
button)

As hardened as Pharaoh

Time to go up tembern hill
(upstairs to bed)

As black as ink

As white as a sheet

As pale as a cloth

As green as a lick (leek)

Gwain like a 'oss in a 'arra
(harrow)

Back like a turf rick

Right as ninepence

A pasty as long as Jan Bedella's
fiddle

Laughing like a piskey

Stiff as a poss (post)

Dead as a door nail

As handy's a showl

Hot as lead

As ragged as Jy weth es shirt hangin' out

Put in weth the bread an' took out weth tha cakes (deficient
person)

As slow as a coach

Prick like a goad (spiked stick)

Clean the corners and the middle will clean itself

Water bewitcht, tea begritcht (weak tea)

Where cobwebs are plentiful kisses are scarce

A stew that do boil is a stew that will spoil

Rough as a downser (bullock on downs)

As light as a gay (broken china)

Warped up like a planchen

As heavy as tin

Vexed as fire

Happy on me awn dung heap (contented person)

As sweet as new hay

A good catch of pilchards meant meat, money and light all in one night

As yalla (yellow) as train (pilchard oil)

Rid round the gills (person crying)

As pluffy as silk

She'll stick her stannin 'ef she don't sell a happorth

Like Mawther's cloamen cat, hollow to his toes

Crock calling the kettle smutty

Hard as nails

You don't need that more than a toad needs side-pockets

He couldn't stop a pig in a passage (bandy legged person)

As old as my little finger and a bit older than my teeth

Nobody will stop their horse from galloping to look at you

Kisses are out of season when gorse is out of bloom

Like a yard of pump water (hair)

Going like Billy o the grinder

The tune the cat died with (shrill song)

Going to the goat's house to see for wool

Naked to the eyes of the world

*Ef yiew wur ti diew as yiew oft to diew, yiew wud
diew a gud deal better than yiew diew diew
(North Cornwall)*

Steamin' like a crock

Dark as a shaft

Small as a croggan

Rubbing through like the heel of a stocking

Looking like a dying duck in a thunderstorm

Carry a knife, a piece of string and some money, you can
    cut, tie, and buy

Do something for your meat if you get your drink for
    nothing

Plum as bun dough

Just between the driftwood and the hard wood (just
    managing to keep going)

Dressed to death like Sally Hatch

Spending money like wildfire (spendthrift)

Sour as a sab (Common sorrel)

Don't see a new penny for an old one (non-paying
    proposition)

Hiding is so bad as stealing (hiding someone else's property)

Like a tom-toddy (or totty) all head and no body

Outward flink, inward stink (outward show)

'Ow be knackin' fore? (How are you?)

He bin awverlooked (illwished)

Can't blaw nor strike (don't know which way to turn)

Off like a star-shot (in a hurry)

Tarred weth the same brush (the same)

Haud ee bal (stop talking)

Laziness edn' wuth nawthun unless 'tes well folleyed

Wash-day Rhymes

PAR

They that wash on Monday, have all the week to dry,
They that wash on Tuesday, are not so much awry
They that wash on Wednesday, are not so much to blame,
They that wash on Thursday, wash for shame,
They that wash on Friday, wash in need,
But they that wash on Saturday, are sluts indeed.

CAMBORNE

She who washes on Monday, has all the week to dry,
She who washes on Tuesday, has soap and starch to buy,
She who washes on Wednesday, is a dainty dame,
She who washes on Thursday, is pretty much the same,
She who washes on Friday, is in need of things indeed,
But she who washes on Saturday, is a careless wife indeed.

ST. AUSTELL

Wash on Monday for health,
Wash on Tuesday for wealth,
Wash on Wednesday, best day of all,
Wash on Thursday for crosses,
Wash on Friday for losses
Wash on Saturday, no luck at all.

A change of work is a as good as a tich-pipe (a rest)
In a proper boil (hot and bothered)
Fit like a stocking on a man's nose
Can't tell A from the track of a duck (stupid person)
Dry as a lime burner's shoe

Beautiful nice like organ broth (made from offal)

Getting married isn't all beer and skittles

He'll wish his cake dough

Laikin' like a basket

Store is no sore

Slept like a ringer

Looking like a tooth drawer

Let the children race over nine lord's land

Forehand pay is the wust of pay

Theer 'tez an' caan't be no 'tezzer'

Like Tommy Dumplens after guldize supper, car' me home
an' don't bend me, for I'm feeling rather passed up

Face like a brandy bottle (red)

You'll live till you die like Nickety Booth

Like Jan Lobb's eyes, hanging in lerrups

All awver alike like a Bryanite (answer to health enquiry)

Turn the best side to London (put best side out)

It's got a silver tail (new thing)

Dumb priests lose their benefits

Time and patience will wear out moor stones or stone postes

He would swear a hole in a iron pot

Quietness is the best noise as Uncle Johnny said when he knocked down his wife

Come easy, go easy

The devil is good to his own

Shut up like a clam

Deep as Dolcoath

Proud as Lucifer

Dressed up to the nines

Promises are like pie crusts, made to be broken

Cold as Greenland

Looking like a stewed owl

Fat as butter

Tough as ling

You'd think she'd been pulled through a furze bush backwards (said of person with unruly hair)

You haven't got your eye in (can't see straight)

Black as the devil's crowst bag (lunch bag)

A derelict mine was referred to as a knackt or scat bal

No catch ee, no 'ave ee

Looking like a white-washed wall (pale person)

All sixties and seventies (in a muddle)

Honest as the sun

Rusty as a handcart

Stale news, hang the scrier

She never said bee nor baw (didn't reply)

She'll live and die in that old thing (favourite garment)

I don't know where 'tis more than the man in the moon

She's a proper whiz (unmanageable)

As crooked as a thorn

As warm as a pie

As rough as a grater

As smooth as new milk

As blunt as a dag (miner's axe)

As keen as a scythe

13

Gone to pot (ruined, no good)

He's a proper limb (limb of the devil) unruly child

An artful maid is stronger than Bolster (Cornish giant)

He edn' wuth his salt (indifferent worker)

She edn' bigger than three-happorth of pence

Big above the shoulders (conceited)

Don't knaw nuff to knaw they don't knaw nothin'

Like some helpers, pulling down with a bar ire (iron) and
   propping up with a stocking needle

She's like a straight Jane from the workhouse

My head don't save my heels (forgetful person)

You wouldn't think butter would melt in her mouth
   (deceptive person)

Strong in the arm, weak in the head

There now, I've ate my words and I aren't no fuller

She'll talk till the cows come home

Going like a lamplighter

Don't know which side their bread is buttered

As dry as a chip

As thin as a willow rod

As clumsy as a beddax (tool for digging)

As smart as a miller taking tolls

As sticky as a dough pan

As plum as a wont (mole) pile

As suant's a fiddle

As hard as iron

As cross as two sticks

As rotten as a pear

Blushing like a piny (peony)

Coming to come like the old woman's butter (nearly finished)

Solid as a barn door

She got brass enough to make a copper kettle

Clemmed to the marra (marrow) feeling cold

No manure can beat the farmer's foot

Mazed as a brush or broom

Animal Sayings

Stinkin' as a polecat

Blind as a bat

Scritchin' like a whitnick (weasel)

Like a bear weth a sore head (vexed person)

Like Farmer Hocking's ducks, more gab than guts

Busted up like a three-halfpenny chick on a wheaten arish (stubble) (after eating too much)

Like an old sheep always seeing greener fields farther on

Live like fighting cocks (folk who live well)

Oal of a hog stog (in a muddle)

Oal of a motion like a Mulfra toad on a rid hot shovel

Cold as a quilkin (frog) or chilled to the marra (marrow)

Clunkin' like a toad (swallowing)

Like Jan Tresize's geese, never happy unless they be wheer they baint

Gwain like a long-dog

Going sideways like a crab going to jail

Like a great buss calf (calf reared on cow) said of a fat young person

Glazin' like a stat (stoat)

Glazin' like a stecked pig

As awkward as a cow with a musket

Like a cat in a bun fire (bonfire)

Ballin' like a Benner bull (Binnerton)

Grulling like a bear with a sore head

A horse with one white foot,
keep it not a day,
A horse with two white feet,
sell it far away,
A horse with three white feet,
sell it to a friend,
A horse with four white feet,
keep it to the end.

A roaring cow do soon forget her calf

Looking as wise as a duck at a thunder cloud

Blawed up like a toad 'pon the dew

Like Nanny Paynter's hens, high upon legs

Wan behind t'other like Scazza mens' ducks (Portscatho)

Everybody to their choice like the old woman when she
kissed the donkey

Graffled up like an arish pig

Like Ludlow's dog leaning agen the wall to bark

The cows got the wap (racing in hot weather)

Fullish as a wagon 'oss

Chittering like a flock of magpies

Daft as a wagon 'oss

Rough as a bear's paw

Taisy as a snake

A toad is a diamond in a duck's eye

Big as bull's beef

All behind like the cow's tail

Like old Jan Keat's 'oss, stagged in the mud

Deef (deaf) as a haddick (haddock)

Sick as a gurnet

As stinkin' as fish

Packed in like herrings in a box

Like a crab going to a christening (going sideways)

White horse, white horse, give me good luck, spit three
times and that's enough

Bit by bit as the cat said when she swallowed the hatchet,
I'll manage it, but it'll be a tight fit

Like an owl looking out of an ivy bush

Everybody do know what to do with a kicking horse except
he that got un (Anne Treneer)

Happy as a duck
Wet as a shag (cormorant)
As yellow as a keet's foot
Thirsty as a gull
A temper like a fowl
As weak as a goose chick
Sick as a shag
Mazed as a curly (curlew)
Wisht as a winnard (red wing)

Tired as a donkey
As fat as a durgey (badger)
As wild as a fitcher (ferret)
As smooth's a bulhorn (snail)
As strong as a 'oss
Blawed up like a wilkie (small toad)
Pleased as a cat with two tails
Dark as a dog's guts
Rough as a badger's back

Weather Sayings

A Saturday moon if it comes once in seven years it comes too soon

Friday's weather is Sunday's weather

Mackerel sky, not twelve hours dry

More rain, more rest, dry weather suits us best

Mist is said to be all for het an' pilchers

Rain before seben, clear before leben

Fire burning blue, sign of cold weather

Smoke going up straight, sign of fine weather, going to ground, sign of rain

If a pig runs round the townplace with straw in its mouth a storm is approaching

Rainbow at morn, put your hook in the corn,
   Rainbow at eve, put your head in the sheave

Haze sign of fine weather, clear vision sign of rain

Fine weather is predicted if there is enough blue sky to make a pair of trousers

Sun cracking the hedges (hot weather)

If the leaves of the trees are blowing upwards it is a sign of rain

Friday and the week seldom alike

See the new moon through glass, you'll have trouble while it lasts

A south-east wind is no good to man nor beast

Mist on the moor, bring sun to the door,

Mist on the hill, bring water to the mill

or

Mist in the valley, bring sun to the alley

Mist on the hill, bring water to the mill

If the ash is in leaf before the oak, then we get a thorough soak
If the oak is in leaf before the ash, then we only get a splash

Rags flying at the grate are known at Mevagissey as 'John Liddicoat's Cobwebs' and are a sign of a gale of wind

"Theer's no 'pendence on the moon" as Uncle Jan Bennetts said when he took a lantern on a moonlit night (mobbing the moon – carrying a lantern in moonlight)

A kettle turned spout inwards indicates a storm at sea

Morning sun in August never last the day

Swallows flying low is a sign of rain

Rain is imminent if rooks fall steeply in flight, or cattle keep close together by a hedge

If spiders are active, fine weather is expected

Larks flying high is another sign, and cattle grazing high on hilly ground

If the cock crows in the door rain will clear

Two full moons in May, neither good for corn nor hay

The harvest will not ripen until after lightning

If Candlemas be fine and clear,
There will be two winters in one year,
But if Candlemas bring clouds and rain,
Winter is gone and will not come again

Crows build high nests in spring if the weather is to be fine, they build in the lower branches of trees if the weather is to be rough

Cat sneezing sign of rain
Aching corn another sign
Bees stay at home in their hives when rain is expected
Rain will follow if the woodpecker calls

If hedgerows produce a lot of berries it means a long hard winter

A sunshine shower will not last an hour

To ensure good luck when you first see the new moon spit on the palm of one hand and cut, or strike, across it with the palm of the other

Prevailing wind for the coming winter will be decided by which quarter the wind is in on All Hallows' Day (1st November)

Pare in May, it grows next day,
Pare in June, you pare too soon,
Pare in July, it's sure to die.

Red sky at night, shepherd's delight
Red sky in the morning, shepherd's warning

Cornish Superstitions

If your left ear burns you are abused, but if you tie a knot in your handkerchief or apron they will bite their tongue

If your right ear burns you are being praised

It is unlucky to burn egg shells

Sew on Saturday sew to the Devil, Saturday should be spent preparing for Sunday

Sew on Good Friday and you will prick the Saviour

Mending clothes on your person indicates a row

If you walk through a house without sitting down you will never go there again

It is unlucky to put the bellows on the table

A man who is cruel to cats will be buried in a storm

It is unlucky to bring May blossom (hawthorn) or furze indoors (or blackthorn)

Never tell your dream before breakfast

Friday's dream Saturday told is sure to come true whate'er behold

Wear green, wear black

It is unlucky to bring old iron into the house

Blackberries should never be picked after the first of October because they have been spat on by the devil

If you put money outdoors on the window-sill on December 31st and bring it in on New Year's Day you will bring in money all the year

A maid-servant who brings in a branch of hawthorn on the first of May is entitled to a dish of cream

At St Just on the first of March it was the custom to brush the doorstep first thing in the morning to brush away all fleas from the house for the ensuing year

The smoke from burning fish is a protection against evil spirits

If the first lamb of the season is an ewe then the farmer's wife is boss for the ensuing year and vice versa

It is unlucky to destroy a colony of ants

A bad tempered person is said to have got out of the bed on the wrong side

It is lucky to fall up the stairs

Spit on money for luck

It is unlucky for two people to look in a mirror at the same time

Seven years trouble ensue if a mirror is broken

Tea leaves on a cup of tea indicate visitors, a long leaf a tall person, a short leaf a short person. Place leaf in the palm and bang with fist counting the days of the week. The day for arrival is when the leaf sticks to the fist

It is unlucky to see the new moon through glass, but if outdoors turn your money and wish

If you break one thing you are sure to break three

It is unlucky to walk under a ladder

You sweep your luck away if you sweep dust out through the doorway

It is unlucky to open an umbrella indoors

If you wash clothes on Innocents' Day you wash one of the family away

Wash blankets in May and you wash one of the family away

It is lucky to pick up a pin with the head turned towards you, unlucky otherwise

22

Fishermen would not go to sea if the vicar, minister, or Salvation Army officer came on the quay, or a woman with a cast in her eye, bad luck would ensue (This can now be counteracted by touching cold iron)

A caul (membrane in which a child is enclosed before birth) was said to be lucky to fishermen. According to an old story, at Cadgwith fishermen would give the donor of a dried caul free fish for life so that good luck would be assured

If you pick sticks on Sunday you will be taken up in the moon

It is lucky to hear the cuckoo for the first time on the right ear, unlucky on the left

Never keep broken cloam or combs

To find a hair or a tyflin (bit of thread) stuck in the mouth is a sign that you will be riled

It is unlucky to put umbrella or shoes on the table

Burn bones and you will hear groans

It is unlucky to lend salt or borrow it

If the rooster crows in the door, visitors can be expected

To ensure a good apple crop place a piece of toast in the fork of the biggest tree in the orchard

Having gone out and forgotten something the person must, on returning, sit in the stairs and count ten

To remove bees on Good Friday will cause them to die

Oxen go down on their knees on Christmas Eve in an attitude of devotion

Mining Superstitions

No miner would ever think of making a cross on a mine because it might offend the knackers (little folk)

A miner named Barker in some way offended the knackers and was crippled by them, hence the saying "As stiff as Barker's knee"

Miners who saw a snail on the way to work dropped a piece of tallow from their candles by its side, bad luck would ensue else

No whistling was allowed underground because it might upset the knackers

Cornish miners believed that muryans were the 'small people' in their state of decay off the earth

To meet a woman on the way to the pit in the middle of the night bad luck will follow

If a miner washes his back he will suffer from weakness in the back

Bad luck of the worst sort will follow a miner who turns back and re-enters his house after leaving for the pit

If you see a miner going to work speak up clearly, lest the missing of this civility should send the man to his labours in haert. The miner might think the passer-by was an ill-wisher if he didn't

If you knock your spoon through the bottom of the shell of a boiled egg no ill luck will befall you

If egg shells are not broken witches will go to sea in them

A loaf of bread upside down indicates a row

Knife falls gentleman calls, fork falls lady calls, spoon falls baby calls

Crossed knives are unlucky

A knife on edge indicates a row

Stir with a knife, you stir up strife

The recipient of a knife as a gift should give the donor a halfpenny to prevent cutting the friendship

Evergreens must be removed from the house before Twelfth Night. It is defying God to burn them; they must be thrown out to decay

To preserve the house from fire take branches of seaweed, dry, and fasten in turned wooden frames and stand on mantelpiece

Red-haired people can never make good butter

Right hand palm itching you will shortly be receiving money. Left hand palm itching you will be paying out money

Nose itching you will be kissed, crossed, or vexed, or shake hands with a fool

Kill a robin or a wran (wren) never prosper boy nor man

When a convalescent person goes out for the first time he must make a circuit of the house with the sun

May cats bring in snakes and adders

Ears ringing, hasty news

The hearthstone should be swept and a basin of spring water left before it for fairies to wash their babies

Never pay out money on a Monday,
or you will pay out all the week
If you receive money on Monday
you will take it in all the week

A robin chirping mournfully means sad news

A hole must be left in one corner of the wall of a house for piskies to come in and out

Wash your face in the dew on May Day to ensure a good complexion

If a person's eyebrows meet they are either deceitful or unlucky

"Rabbits" should be the first word spoken on the first day of the month

Bad luck will follow the spilling of salt unless some is thrown over the left shoulder

A branch of an ash tree will keep away snakes

Quarrels in the house will ensue if gravy is poured out of a spoon backwards

It is unlucky to meet on the stairs

Put on the left stocking first for good luck

If fire won't kindle your husband is in a bad temper

If you drop your umbrella or gloves it is unlucky to pick them up yourself, if someone else picks them up they will get a surprise

The fire hook and prong should be crossed to keep out witches

The brandis (trivet) should be turned down on the baking iron to prevent the small folk sitting on it

Cut corns when the moon is waning to prevent them growing again

Cut hair when the moon is full to prevent it falling out

Cross a stile and a gate hardby you'll be a widow before you die

Picking dandelions was said to induce bed-wetting. The penalty was a mouse pasty

A deserted maiden should steal her lover's jacket, turn the sleeves inside-out and bury it in the churchyard at night. The lover's heart will turn as the jacket rots until he comes back repentant to his old flame

You will be shortly be receiving money if there are bubbles on your tea

House leek planted on the roof will preserve the place from lightning

Rabbits and pigs must not be mentioned when fishermen go to sea

It is unlucky to eat pilchards from head downwards, eating from tail to head brings fish to the shore

If you place a piece of tin in a bank of muryans (ants) at a certain stage of the moon it will turn to silver

Good blackberry season, good herring season

Blackberry stains will not disappear while the fruit is in season

It is said that hair falls out in the blackberry season

A scow tree (elder) keeps away evil spirits

Where a bay tree grows the house will never have a fire

A pot of shamrock growing in the house is most unlucky

A sign of a quarrel is to wash in the same water as some other person. To avert this make the sign of a cross over the water

> The sight of one magpie is a
> sign of anger
> Two sign of mirth
> Three sign of marriage
> Four sign of birth
> Five for silver
> Six for gold
> Seven for a secret that must
> never be told
>
> *Another variation*
> One's sorrow,
> Two's mirth,
> Three's a wedding,
> Four's a birth
> Five's a christening,
> Six a death,
> Seven's heaven,
> Eight is hell,
> Nine the devil his-self

A stranger in your house on Christmas Day means bad luck
in the following year

If you are served with half a cup of tea, it is a sign that you
will be a widower

Servants coming in a new situation on a Saturday or after
mid-day dinner do not stay long

Whistling by night is unlucky to fishermen

Cubyleek or cactus, as its spikes grow, so your troubles will
grow with them

White geraniums or white pelargoniums bring poor luck

A hole in the fire indicates a death

It is unlucky to keep plants in a bedroom

It is unlucky to sit thirteen at a table

Never start a fresh job on a Friday

It is unlucky to watch a friend go out of sight through a window

A ginger cat is a charm against fire

Sunday's moon the sailor's dread

It is unlucky to mend your own gloves. This does not apply to mending other people's gloves

Sunday's plans never come true

It is unlucky to sit in the stairs, to cut butter or bread both ends, or sit on the table

Busts or statues or other figures are poor luck to bring indoors

When planting a flower or plant in order that it may flouish always tell it your name and say – "Grow for....."

It is unlucky to cut an elder tree or its blossom without first asking its permission or apologising to the spirit of the tree

Accidentally leave off the cover of a teapot or kettle and if you can't find it, a stranger is coming to the house

If a piece of bread falls to the floor bread will be cheaper. If when making a gift it falls to the floor, the present will be sure to please

To dream of fruit out of season means anger without reason

Mirrors should be covered when there is lightning

Doors should be left open in a thunderstorm

Starting with the thumb the rhyme went as follows:

Gift, friend, foe, true lover to come, journey to go

Cut your nails on Monday for news (it could be bad news)

On Tuesday for a new pair of shoes

On Wednesday for a letter

On Thursday for something better

On Friday for sorrow

On Saturday see your fair true love tomorrow

On Sunday the Devil will be with you all the week

When you hear the cuckoo for the first time in spring, if it calls twelve times in succession you will not want for bread for the rest of the year

If the first lambs of the season are looking towards you that is a sign of good luck

If the bottom of your foot itches you will walk on strange ground

White specks on nails presage good fortune, black specks misfortune

Birth Superstitions

If more than one lady pours from the teapot there may be family increases

A footling baby has magical gifts

The 7th child of a 7th child has second sight

Moving houses may be the cause of an increase in the family

The eating of skate accounts for large families

A dog fish eaten in the month of May secures a male heir

A child born from a Caesarian operation has unusual strength and the ability to see spirits and discover hidden treasure

Early death is predicted if the child is born in the interval between the old and the new moon

May children are thought to be weakly

Weighing babies was considered unlucky

Babies should not be tucked on a weekday

If a baby cries long he will live long

A child should not be named after a dead brother or sister

If you give away baby clothes you will need them again

Brushing the child's foot with a rabbit's foot is supposed to bring good luck

A baby should walk before it talks

Babies were given silver as a symbol of purity

Tickling the child's foot will make it stammer

Rock the cradle empty, you'll rock babies plenty

If a child is born on the wane of the moon the next birth will be of the opposite sex

If a birth takes place at the growing of the moon the next child will be of the same sex

It was considered unlucky to wash a baby's head until it was 12 months old

By washing dirt out of the creases of the child's hands one would wash away riches

It was the custom to light candles at birth and at death to ward off evil spirits

To ensure easy birth or death all the doors and windows of the house should be open and lying on the floor was also considered helpful

It was thought that birth marks took the shape of something which frightened the mother before the birth, or something that she fancied to eat (like a strawberry, etc)

A cradle should never be made or mended with elder wood as it is thought that the Cross was made from this tree

A child's name should never be told before the christening

Babies were christened at an early age otherwise the baby might not go to heaven if it died

Baptism was thought to benefit ailing children

Holy water was begged from the priest, and church fonts were kept locked

If a child cries at the christening it means that the Devil has been driven out, but if the child does not cry it is said to be too good to live

Nail clippings, hair toppings, and teeth were always burnt to prevent them falling into the hands of a witch

If teeth weren't burned the child might have dog's teeth

A baby's nails must be bitten for the first year and not cut or the child will grow up to be a thief

At baptisms boys should be christened before girls to prevent them from becoming too 'womanish'; girls would be too boyish if christened first

'First at the font, never at the altar' was said of a young couple who were godparents at a christening, but others said it was a sure sign that they would become sweethearts

If you show a blue vein on the bridge of your nose, You'll never survive to wear wedding clothes

From marriages in May, bairns die and decay

Tuck babies in May, you'll tuck them in clay

To dream of a baby is a terrible dream, it foretells trouble

Sunday's child is full of grace,
Monday's child is fair of face,
Tuesday's child is solemn and sad,
Wednesday's child is merry and glad,
Thursday's child is inclined to thieving,
Friday's child is free in giving,
Saturday's child works hard for his living

Another variation is as follows;
Monday's child is fair of face,
Tuesday's child is full of grace,
Wednesday's child is full of woe,
Thursday's child had far to go,
Friday's child is loving and giving,
Saturday's child works hard for its living,
But the child that is born on the Sabbath Day
Is blithe and bonny, good and gay

Wedding Superstitions

Place a piece of wedding cake under your pillow and you will dream of your future husband

Write three names on separate pieces of paper, roll them up tightly, and place each in a separate ball of earth. Drop balls into a basin of water and the first name to be seen as the ball unrolls is that of your spouse

To make sure of your lover wear some of his or her hair in a locket

Valentine's Day and hempseed. At St Ives girls would gather in a ring and scatter hemp seed to raise the wraith of the future husbands repeating this verse -

Hempseed I sow, Hempseed grow,

And he who my true love will be,

Come after me and mow

A girl sometimes presents her fiancé with a knife to break off the engagement

It is unlucky to have the banns published on Sundays which are in different years

Three times a bridesmaid never a bride

It is unlucky for a single person to try on a wedding ring

Marry in May you'll rue it for aye

It is considered lucky if the new initials spell a word

It is unlucky for two sisters to marry two brothers

A courting couple photographed together will never marry

It is unlucky to be married on your birthday

Marry in Lent you may live to repent

It is unlucky to sign anything with the new name before the wedding

The white of a new-laid egg placed in a glass of water and exposed to the sun before noon on a midsummer day will assume a shape that foretells the occupation of one's future partner

You will marry the man with whom you walk over Newlyn bridge

Myrtle put under the pillow will bring fortunate dreams, an un-married woman will dream of her future husband

On All Hallow's Eve in order to dream of your future husband repeat aloud as you place your shoes in the form of a letter T at the foot of the bed — "I cross my shoes in the form of a T, hoping this night my true love to see". Then get into bed backwards and don't speak afterwards

"St Simon and St Jude, may I intrude and tell me the name of my lover". Repeat this and throw the unbroken skin of a peeled apple over the left shoulder, when the initial letter of the name will be formed by the peel

If a girl sits on a table when talking to a man she will never marry

The wedding outfit in full must not be put on before the wedding day and it is unlucky for the bride to look in the mirror with her veil on

The bridegroom must not see the bride until they meet at the church

Married in white, you have chosen aright;
Married in grey, you will go far away;
Married in black, you will wish yourself back;
Married in red you will wish yourself dead;
Married in green, ashamed to be seen;
Married in blue, he will always be true;
Married in pearl, you will live in a whirl;
Married in yellow, ashamed of your fellow;
Married in brown, you will live out of town;
Married in pink, your spirits will sink

It is lucky to meet a sweep when going to or coming from the church, and to be kissed by one is even more lucky

The bride must step into church on the right foot

It is unlucky for the couple to hear their banns read, if they do their first child is likely to be an idiot

It is lucky for the bride to hear a cat sneeze on her wedding eve, or be awakened by the song of birds on the morn of the wedding

Good fortune is ensured by making part of her trousseau, but not the wedding dress

Pins used in the dresses were always thrown away by the bridesmaids to prevent bad luck, and if a bridesmaid kept a pin it meant she wouldn't marry for a year and might even be an old maid

It is lucky if an even number attends the ceremony

It is unlucky for the couple to enter the church by one door and leave by another

To see a black cat on the way to church is considered fortunate, or if a black cat rubs itself against the bride

A spider is an emblem of money and prosperity and good luck is foreshadowed if the bride finds one in the folds of her wedding dress

It is unlucky if the wedding ring is dropped during the service, or if it is lost or broken

The bridesmaid who catches the bouquet tossed by the bride will be the next to wed

An old boot and tin pots and pans were tied to the vehicle in which the 'weddiners' rode after the ceremony

The bride should be carried over the threshold of her new home

Blessed is the bride whom the sun shines on,

Blessed is the dead that the rain rains on

If it rains while the wedding party is on its way to church, or returning, a life of bickering and unhappiness may be expected

When December snow falls fast, marry and true love will last

Four spoons sign of a wedding

Do not put a folded handkerchief in your pocket, that will mean pure'n bad luck – you will not be married

Windows of the new home were sometimes white-washed and chimneys blocked. In parts of Cornwall a shillalley band (group of young folk with pots and pans) serenaded the young pair when they arrived and often invaded the house

The bride must wear something old, and something new,
Something borrowed and something blue

(Something old to remind her of her old friends, and blue is considered a lucky colour)

It is unlucky to get married on a Friday, but Sunday is a good day

Change the name and not the letter,

Change for worse and not for better

"Even ash I thee do carry in my hand,
Hoping thus to meet the man
Who shall be my husband.
If he be married let him pass by,
If he be single, let him draw nigh"

Monday for wealth,
Tuesday for health,
Wednesday the best day of all.
Thursday for losses,
Friday for crosses,
And Saturday, no luck at all

Funeral Superstitions

If rain falls on a coffin the soul of the departed has arrived safely

After a death flower pots should be draped with crèpe to prevent the plants from dying

Bees should be told of a death and the hives draped with crepe. Bird cages were also draped with crepe

The falling of a picture was a warning of death within a month, especially to the person by whom it fell

Making of a will was said to portend early death to the testator

If a person shivered it was said that someone was walking over the place where their grave will be

A man who is cruel to cats will have terrible weather at his funeral or be buried in a storm

To return to a house in which you have previously lived denotes bad luck or death

It was thought to be unlucky to walk on a grave

The bed should be athurt the planchen (floor) for death to come easily

A hole in a loaf of bread indicates a grave

Never carry a corpse to church by a new road

It used to be said that if a corpse was carried over a private road the ground became a right of way

A corpse must be buried with its feet towards the east

Suicides were not taken into church before burial

Always touch a corpse that you may see to avoid always seeing it before you

Transplanting parsley is a sign of a death in the family

Holes in bread sign of the death of a friend

To have the 'tie' turned while ill in bed means death for the patient

To dream of the dead you hear of the living

To dream of someone else liming or of liming yourself is a sure sign of a death

If you dream of a wedding you will hear of a death

To hear the sound of water dripping, when actually there is no water, is a sure sign of death

Arum lilies or trumpet lilies are known as devil's candles and are associated with poor luck perhaps from their being used for wreaths

A robin tapping at a window was a warning of trouble

If a robin came into the house it was a sure sign that a fatal illness would attack one of the family shortly

If a cock crows at midnight the angel of death is passing over

A raven croaking over a house bodes ill to some member of the family

Cornish Remedies

Mortals are we and subject to diseases,
We must all die, even and when God pleases,
Into the world but one way do we come,
A thousand ways from thence we are sent home

Medicine with good 'seddlement' is best

A tooth from a dead man's mouth is an infallible charm if carried in the pocket

No more toothache for a year if a nail is driven into an oak tree, or if the first fern to appear in the Spring is bitten from the ground

Another cure is to catch a frog, open its mouth, spit into it, and cast the frog away. Pepper rubbed into the gums will allay the pain

To keep away evil spirits from cattle, nail four horse shoes in the form of a cross against the door

To cure colic stand on one's head for a quarter of an hour

To cure heartache sleep with the key of the church door around your neck

Formula for toothache

"Upon a rock St Peter stood, towards Jerusalem. And Peter prayed, Lord, forgive me my sins, and I shall be free. In the name of the Father, and of the Son, and of the Holy Ghost, Amen".
(Say three times a day, three days running, and drink powdered brimstone water between whiles)

To cure warts steal a piece of meat, run it over the warts and bury it, or pick a peapod with nine peas, throw away the ninth pea, saying, 'wart, wart, dry away'. As the pea rots warts disappear. A piece of turf can also be used. Or you can take as many pebbles as you have warts and touch each wart with corresponding pebbles. Wrap stones in cloth or paper and throw away in the road, or lose them on the way to church. Whoever picks them up will have the warts. Rub warts with fasting spittle is another remedy. Never wash your hands in water an egg has been boiled in, you'll get warts

Black spiders dried and powered cure heartburn

Water taken from the church font is good for children with rickets and will straighten bow-legged children and children with the wobbles

Sacrifices of live animals were made to prevent cattle dying

A live pigeon was cut in half to cure a sick woman, the bleeding parts put to her feet

To cure the thrush in a child take it fasting on three mornings following to have its mouth blown into by a person who never knew his father, or take three rushes from a running stream and pass them separately through the mouth of the infant. Then plunge the rushes in the stream, and as the current bears them away the thrush will leave the child. The 8th psalm read three times a day three days following was also said to cure the thrush

To cure boils creep on hands and knees beneath a bramble
  grown into soil at both ends, or bore a hole in a nutmeg
  and tie round your neck and nibble nine mornings
  fasting and boils will disappear

Breathe over a newly made grave to cure a cough

To cure a tumour place on it the hand of a man who has
  committed suicide

Children who cannot retain their water can be cured by
  eating roasted mice

To cure shingles take the blood drawn from a cat's tail and
  smear over the affected part

Bruise an ivy leaf and wrap round
  the toe to cure a corn, or tie a
  piece of fat bacon round it

A muslin bag full of spiders tied
  round patient's neck is also
  said to cure whooping cough

Take a spoonful of earth from the
  grave of a newly interred
  virgin, dissolve in water, and
  drink fasting to cure decline
  (tuberculosis)

Children who are sick after
  whooping cough should run
  with the sheep

The dead body of an adder,
  bruised on the wound it has made is an infallible cure for
  its bite

Boiled onion placed in a stocking will cure earache

Tea made from dried camomile flowers will cure an upset
  stomach

Drop a key inside clothing at the back to cure nose bleeding

Vinegar and honey will help cure a cough

*Miners used to believe
that mundic applied
to a cut would cure
it, and they always
liked to wash an
injury in water
which ran through
mundic ore*

For a scald or a burn gather nine bramble leaves and put them into a vessel of clear spring water. Pass each leaf over the scald and repeat three times to each leaf, "Three came from the east, one with fire, and two with frost, out with thee, fire, and in with thee, frost, in the name of the Father, Son, and Holy Ghost"

If a fisherman cuts himself he takes a lobworm from his bait and presses it on the wound, then throws worm in water and washes cut in water

Charmers can stop bleeding. They cannot accept money, and the patient must not say thank you. Secrets for charming can only be handed down to the opposite sex. Sometimes a cure can be effected without the charmer seeing the patient. A boy was cured of asthma by sending the charmer his vest six times. A white witch breathed, blew and muttered strange words over warts to cure them

To cure asthma roll spider webs in a ball and swallow them

A church key applied to a wound stops bleeding, or else cover the wound with cobwebs

The sign of a cross drawn on wood, stone, or metal and bound over a wound stops bleeding in man or beast

A stye on the eye is cured by stroking nine times with a wedding ring or a tom cat's tail

A baby should wear a coral necklace to ensure easy teething

Toad's liver fried is good for rheumatism, as also are adders' tails. The adders must be killed whilst the dew is on them. A cabbage leaf wrapped round the affected part is also said to be a cure. Some folks carry a cork, potato, or nutmeg in their pocket, or a piece of mountain ash

Fair people should wash their hair in camomile liquor. The dried camomile flowers should be steeped in boiling water and strained when cool

To cure whooping cough eat a piece of cake belonging to a married couple called John and Joan, or gather nine stones from a stream, also a quart of water (not taken against the flow) make stones red hot, put in the water and bottle. Give child a wineglassful nine mornings running

Another cure – find female donkey, three years old, draw child naked nine times over the animal's back and under its belly. Draw three spoonfuls of milk from donkey's teats, cut three hairs from back and belly and put in milk. Stand for three hours to acquire proper virtue. Give child to drink and repeat process three successive mornings. At Sancreed as late as 1883 a girl with whooping cough was passed nine times under a donkey's belly from a man on one side to a woman on the other, a boy meanwhile feeding the animal with 'cribs'

For sciatica carry either a knuckle bone of a leg of mutton, a raw potato, a piece of lodestone or a nutmeg in a pocket, or round the neck

Cut off cat's ear (left one) and swallow three drops of blood in a wineglass of spring water, claimed by white witch as a cure for measles

45

> *Boosening is a cure for madness, the person is immersed in water until on the point of drowning, and repeated if necessary, (associated with Altarnun)*

Club moss is good for eye diseases. On the third day of the moon, when crescent is seen for the first time, show it knife to be used for cutting the moss saying "As Christ healed the issue of blood, do thou cut what thou cuttest for good". At sundown wash hands, kneel, cut moss, wrap it in white cloth and boil in water from spring nearest its growth. Use for bathing eyes

To cure goitre, go before sunrise on the first day of May to the grave of last young man buried in the churchyard, pass hand three times from head to foot of grave and apply dew collected to part affected

To cure 'hiccups' wet the forefinger of the right hand with spittle and cross the front of the left shoe three times saying the Lord's Prayer backwards. Frightening the affected person is another remedy

Rub stings from nettles with a dock leaf

Ointment for bruises was made from bruised mallow leaves mixed with lard, or treated by applying the convex side of a tablespoon. Apply a bread poultice to a whitlow

A few drops of nitre on a lump of sugar for curing bladder trouble

Place a half-crown piece on a bleeding ulcer in the leg and secure it to stop bleeding

Bathe feet in mustard water for a cold and drink boiled cider, or whisky with hot water and sugar. Elder tea made from dried elder flowers or leaves was another cure, or drink the juice from turnip slices with sugar between

Stand ankle in cold water for a sprain

Soak a handkerchief in vinegar and place on forehead to relieve headache

A few drops of Friar's Balsam on a 'knub' of sugar will help a cold or inhale same in hot water with a towel over the head

Rub a bad back with an empty bottle

Put red flannel or brown paper on the chest to relieve bronchitis. Red flannel was always thought to contain more healing properties

Sit on a hot cushion to cure diarrhoea

Weakly children were bathed in Mennacuddle Well

Uncle Jacky Hooper, of Blowing House, Redruth, cured sick cows by giving the owner a prayer, or chapter to read from Proverbs. To be read over the animal's back. Charge 5/-

To cure a sore throat, sleep with a stocking from the left leg around your throat

To cure rheumatism boil a ha'p'orth of mustard in a pint of beer. An old lady said she had taken 27 quarts and it had done her a power of good

Dragon's blood, (bright red gum exuding from kind of palm tree) was said to be used in medicine

Take enough sulphur to cover a sixpence to keep the blood in order

For neuralgia put a plaster of fresh cow dung to the face

Rub butter on a bruise

Smear goose fat on a brown paper plaster for a chest cold

To cure chilblains, dip the affected part in the charlie (chamber pot)

For curing infantile mesenteric disease (stomach illness) children were taken to Chapel Euny Well, Sancreed, and washed on first three Wednesdays in May, then drawn through pool three times against the sun and three times on surrounding grass. People suffering from humour and wounds were also supposed to be cured here